Noah's Ark

A Play

Colin and Mary Crowther

A SAMUEL FRENCH ACTING EDITION

SAMUELFRENCH-LONDON.CO.UK
SAMUELFRENCH.COM

Copyright © 2001 by Colin Crowther and Mary Crowther
All Rights Reserved

NOAH'S ARK is fully protected under the copyright laws of the British Commonwealth, including Canada, the United States of America, and all other countries of the Copyright Union. All rights, including professional and amateur stage productions, recitation, lecturing, public reading, motion picture, radio broadcasting, television and the rights of translation into foreign languages are strictly reserved.

ISBN 978-0-573-06255-1

www.samuelfrench-london.co.uk

www.samuelfrench.com

FOR AMATEUR PRODUCTION ENQUIRIES

UNITED KINGDOM AND WORLD EXCLUDING NORTH AMERICA
plays@SamuelFrench-London.co.uk
020 7255 4302/01

Each title is subject to availability from Samuel French, depending upon country of performance.

CAUTION: Professional and amateur producers are hereby warned that NOAH'S ARK is subject to a licensing fee. Publication of this play does not imply availability for performance. Both amateurs and professionals considering a production are strongly advised to apply to the appropriate agent before starting rehearsals, advertising, or booking a theatre. A licensing fee must be paid whether the title is presented for charity or gain and whether or not admission is charged.

The professional rights in this play are controlled by Samuel French Ltd, 52 Fitzroy Street, London, W1T 5JR.

No one shall make any changes in this title for the purpose of production. No part of this book may be reproduced, stored in a retrieval system, or transmitted in any form, by any means, now known or yet to be invented, including mechanical, electronic, photocopying, recording, videotaping, or otherwise, without the prior written permission of the publisher. No one shall upload this title, or part of this title, to any social media websites.

The right of Colin and Mary Crowther to be identified as author of this work has been asserted by them in accordance with Section 77 of the Copyright, Designs and Patents Act 1988

CHARACTERS

Noah
Mrs Noah
Shem
Mrs Shem
Ham
Mrs Ham
Japheth
Mrs Japheth
Chorus of Nasty Neighbours (who also act out the sounds of the storm)
Chorus of Animals (who also act out the voice of **God**)

Location: far away

Time: long ago

This play was first performed in 1995 by Dovetail Theatre School.

PRODUCTION NOTES

It is hoped that with the aid of these notes and the stage directions given in the script, even the least experienced director will feel enabled to produce an effective piece of theatre with minimal cost and effort. More confident directors should feel free to add music (to open and close the play), and special effects (for the rising water and the rainbow), but these should be kept short or they will swamp a play that derives its strength from its simplicity. The production has been designed to make good use of the very first acting lessons you will have given the children: how to freeze (to stand very still but completely relaxed); how to mime actions (building the Ark); how to use the voice to speak as a chorus and to create the sounds of the weather; and how to mime movements while standing on the spot (walking, running, swimming). These simple techniques give this play its unique dramatic style.

The play was written to be performed by a group of twenty to thirty 7-10 year olds. There are three groups of characters in the play: Noah's family, their Nasty Neighbours and the Animals. The family all have dialogue and actions to perform. The neighbours mainly mime their roles and create the sounds of the weather. The animals also speak in chorus as the voice of God. When speaking God's words, the children can either speak simultaneously, or you could divide the lines between different speakers and only have them speak together a few key lines. Either way, they should portray God as friendly, encouraging, and passionately concerned about his creation, and not some frightening, bullying ghost.

All the actors are on stage all the time. They sit in a semi-circle, facing into the action and watching what is happening. When their turn comes, they simply get up from their places, perform in the central acting area and then return to their places in the semi-circle.

This will be found to aid the pace of the play and the concentration of the performers. The actors should all wear the same—a plain dark track suit and bare feet or dance shoes—not trainers! A plain, light-coloured stole pinned to Noah's shoulders will add to the feeling that he has been singled out for God's special attention. All the props should be mimed. The Ark is created using a long, boat-shaped piece of brown cloth, which the actors will hold up. It is stored R of the platform. The dove can be a simple cardboard cut-out, mounted on a short pole and operated by one of the performers as a rod-puppet, without any attempt to conceal the operator. It is stored L of the platform. The rainbow effect can be created with swathes of coloured cloth, tied at one end to the top of an unseen ladder and unfurled by the animals across the back of the stage, where they hold it in place until the play is over, or by using a very large paper fan, painted in the colours of the rainbow. Similarly, if you want to create the effect of rising water, then use long strips of thin material, dyed different shades of blue. If five or six of these are thrown across the forestage as the rain starts, and held at each end by the animals, or by any spare actors, they can be rippled and lowered to suggest the rising and falling water levels. But the real effect of the sea is created by the actors' imaginations, so it would be unwise to expend too much effort or time on these effects.

The play is designed for thrust-stage presentation, (with the audience on three sides of the stage), but would work equally well in the round or on an end-stage. There is a bare platform UC which serves both as Noah's house and, later, as the Ark. It should be big enough for all the family and all the animals to stand on without overcrowding. The main acting area is a semi-circle, C. (See the groundplan in the Furniture and Property List.) A cyclorama would be useful but is not essential. There is no need to attempt to reproduce realistic lighting effects. Simple cover lighting is all that is necessary. Any music—and all sound effects—should be produced live by the actors. This way the actors learn their true job—to create a world of the imagination on stage which they believe in so intently that the audience can share in it too.

Colin and Mary Crowther

AUTHORS' NOTES

We have contracted the episode with the dove for dramatic purposes, just as the original writer lengthened his version—compared with the extant versions of the story in Babylonian and Sumerian traditions—and used repetition for narrative effect. For example, in the Bible, the Flood lasts 150 days, but in our version, about fifteen minutes. Similarly, Noah sends out a raven, waits a week, sends out the dove, waits a week, sends out the dove again and it returns with the olive leaves, waits a week, sends out the dove again and this time it does not return. In theatrical terms this would take too long to show. So in our version it goes out once and comes back with the olive branch. We believe therefore that our version is dramatically faithful to the original and still in line with the narrator's aim: to show the power of God and Noah's faith in God.

Theologians have identified two writers to this strand of *Genesis* whom they call the Priestly writer and the Yahwist. This explains why occasionally, there are two versions (as in the story of Creation) or, as here, why the text appears to contradict itself. In 8:7b, Noah sent out the dove seven days after the "water upon the earth had dried up" (so the ark must have hit dry—or rather, very wet—ground). The dove could not find anywhere to settle—doves settle in trees not on the ground. Seven days later he tried again and the dove brought back the olive branch. Seven days later it flew away and never returned. By this point, according to verse 13b "the surface of the ground was dry". We make that point: it is muddy, it dries up. The dove goes out between these two stages. Our version, we hope, makes sense of the biblical narrative; is in line with current theological exegesis of the text; and makes for effective theatre.

Colin and Mary Crowther

NOAH'S ARK

At a given signal the actors file on in two lines, from UR *and* UL

They take up their positions as described on the groundplan and sit, cross-legged, in a semi-circle, facing the central acting area. As they do so, the Lights in the auditorium go down and the Lights on stage come up. If there is to be music, they could sing two verses at this point

Then Noah rises and his family follow him, up on to the platform. This now becomes their house. It has an (invisible) central door on either side of which is a shuttered window. Noah opens the door to let them in and closes it behind them. They lie down to sleep. Noah's three sons lie L *of the platform, heads outward, and their wives lie* R. *Noah and Mrs Noah then lie down* C, *at the front of the platform, their heads* DS. *They all sleep, quiet and still*

An owl is heard. Noah is restless and turns over, in his sleep, on to his back. At first, the word of God is heard as a whisper, echoed by each of the animals in turn

God Noah!

Noah wakes up and turns to face his wife

Noah What is it, my dear?
Mrs Noah Nothing, go back to sleep.

Noah turns over and goes back to sleep

God (*louder now*) Noah!

Noah wakes up, stretches and sits up

Noah How can I sleep on such a beautiful morning? (*He rises, comes forward, opens the window shutters and looks out. He is very happy*)

A cock crows

Look at the world! What a beautiful place it is!

Mrs Noah wants to go back to sleep

Mrs Noah And look at the mess our neighbours have made of it!
Noah But this could be the dawn of a new age.
Mrs Noah You say that every day.
Noah And every day it could be true.
Mrs Noah Go back to sleep.
God (*all the animals speaking together, very firmly*) Noah!
Noah Is … that … you … Lord?
God Look at the people I made.

Noah opens the door and stands looking down into the marketplace, c. The Nasty Neighbours begin to stir, to stretch and yawn and scratch. Then they begin to get ready for the morning market

A farmer goes out to his field and cuts the cabbages which his son loads on to his handcart, but it is clear from the way the son wrinkles his nose that some of them are not very fresh. Never mind, they all go in

A mother rolls out pieces of dough and tosses them carelessly to her daughter, who catches the first one and drops it into the frying-pan, but misses the second one, then burns the first one trying to catch the third one. Mother picks up the second one, brushes off the dirt and tosses that in the pan. Never mind, they all go in

Noah's Ark

A merchant counts his pile of silver coins. One is clearly a fake and bends when he bites it. But he puts it back in the pile and smiles at the thought of the even bigger pile of money he'll be counting tomorrow

A sly young thief sharpens an evil-looking knife and, when he is sure no-one is looking, hides it under his jacket, with an even more evil smile

Two children, sent out to hitch the donkey to the cart, are clearly in a bad mood and are very rough with the donkey ... in other words, though each Neighbour performs a different mime, because all the mimes are happening at the same time, we see that they are all greedily thinking how they can get the better of their other neighbours today

Noah (*pointing*) I see them, Lord, down there in the market-place.

The Nasty Neighbours come forward into the market, some to sell and some to buy ... all to cheat, all with a false smile on their greedy faces ... but the donkey refuses to budge. Their parents give the children responsible a clip round the ear and they are left to tug and push the stubborn donkey while everyone else goes off to market

God Look, Noah. Look hard.

The Nasty Neighbours begin to buy and sell. A beautiful fresh cabbage attracts a poor widow, but the one put in her bag, she soon realizes, has gone bad

A hungry young man buys a lovely hot pie, but when he bites into it, he discovers a long hair in it

One stall-holder is delighted with the silver coin he gets from the merchant—but suspicious when he bites it and it bends

And the merchant won't be laughing long when he realizes the thief has sliced through the strings of his purse and relieved him of all his money ... and the angry children beat the poor donkey

What do you see, Noah, my friend?

The Nasty Neighbours freeze

Noah Well, they're not very kind, not very honest, not very gentle with——
Animal 1 (*as voice of God*) They are greedy!
Animal 2 (*as voice of God*) They are selfish!
Animal 3 (*as voice of God*) They are cruel!
Animal 4 (*as voice of God*) They steal, they cheat, they hurt!

Quickly, the Nasty Neighbours return to their places in the semi-circle

Noah But you made them, Lord.
God And I shall unmake them.

Noah steps down from the platform, amazed. He looks straight in front of him when he is talking to God, as if God is only a few feet away and slightly taller than him

Noah What do you mean, Lord?
God I shall just have to start all over again.
Noah What? Destroy everyone? Man, woman and child?
God Everyone.
Noah And the animals? The birds? Even the creepy-crawlies?
God Every single one.
Noah Then who will be left, Lord, to praise your name?

Short pause

God You, Noah, my faithful friend.

Short pause

Noah's Ark 5

Noah Me?
God Now listen. Here's what I want you to do.

Noah kneels in prayer. With his eyes shut and his face lifted, he listens carefully to God, reacting occasionally to what God tells him. Mrs Noah wakes up and rises. She comes to the door of her house and calls out to her husband

Mrs Noah Noah, dear. It's time to… (*Realizing he is praying, Mrs Noah tiptoes back into the house, closing the door behind her. Then she goes over to her sleeping family*) Boys, wake up! Shem, Ham, Japheth!

But her sons do not stir. Mrs Noah sighs—same as usual! She wakes their wives, who get up at once

Come on, girls. It's up to us again, I see. (*She gives directions to each wife*) Fetch the water. Grind the flour. Bake the bread.

The wives set about their tasks

And quietly—don't disturb Noah—he's praying.
Wife 1 (*drawing a bucket of water from the well*) Noah's always praying.
Wife 2 (*grinding the flour*) I dread to think what the neighbours will say.

Mrs Noah blows on the embers of the fire, then stirs the pot of vegetables hanging above it, tasting it to check it is ready. Wife 3 clears a space on the table. Wife 2 empties a pile of flour on to it and makes a hole in the middle. Wife 1 pours some water into the hole. Wife 3 begins to knead the flour. It is hard work, but all the women work as a team and it is clear they do this every day

Wife 3 It's embarrassing, that's what it is.

They each take a piece of dough, roll it out very thin, then pass their dough along the line to Mrs Noah

Mrs Noah (*flipping the unleavened bread over on the fire*) It's better than lying in bed all day!

The wives queue up to take a hot piece of the bread from Mrs Noah, then add a spoonful of vegetables from the pot, wrap it up like a parcel, then take the food to their sleeping husbands. Mrs Noah makes up her own breakfast and sits on the step outside her house, eating it quietly and enjoying the early morning sunshine

Wife 1 Here, Shem! Eat.
Wife 2 Here, Ham! Drink.
Wife 3 Japheth! Japheth!

Japheth wakes up in a very grumpy mood

Be merry!

Shem and his wife move LC of the platform and sit on the floor to eat their breakfast. Ham and his wife move UC of the platform. Japheth and his wife stay where they are. Japheth goes back to sleep. His wife eats alone. Meanwhile, Mrs Noah finishes her breakfast, wipes her hands on her (invisible) apron and comes forward to her husband. Noah, though, is still talking to God

Mrs Noah Noah?
Noah An ark, Lord? Are you sure, Lord? (*He listens, then sighs*) Whatever you say, Lord.
Mrs Noah Husband? You must eat.
Noah No time now, my dear. I must build an ark. (*He marches back towards the house*)

Mrs Noah thinks about this

Mrs Noah (*calling after him*) Noah, you can't even build a bench!
Noah (*turning back to her*) Then you must help me. We must all work together.

Noah's Ark

Mrs Noah, very puzzled, walks up to him

Mrs Noah To build an Ark?
Noah Yes. The girls can make the sail——
Mrs Noah You mean—a ship?
Noah Yes. The boys can cut the wood——
Mrs Noah You mean—a ship to sail the sea?
Noah Yes. And I'll fix it all together. (*He climbs the platform step, as if to enter his house*)

Mrs Noah catches him by the sleeve and gently pulls him back outside

Mrs Noah Noah, Noah, my dear, the sea is hundreds of miles away. Why, it's twenty miles through the forest to the nearest lake!
Noah That reminds me. You can go to the forest and collect the animals. (*He turns back to the house, climbs the step and opens the door*)
Mrs Noah Animals?
Noah Yes. The girls can feed and water them——
Mrs Noah You mean—wild animals?
Noah Yes. The boys can clean out their cages.
Mrs Noah Noah... Noah, my dear... (*It is all too much for her and she sits on the step*)

Noah comes down and sits beside her

Noah Trust me.
Mrs Noah Yes, my dear. I do, my dear.

He puts his arm around her shoulder. They remain very still, while inside the house:

Shem I'm bored.
Ham So am I.
Japheth I'm bored, bored, bored!
Shem There's never anything interesting to do around here.

Ham Just the same old routine, day in, day out...
Japheth Seed-time and harvest...
Ham Summer and winter...
Shem Nothing exciting ever happens. This must be the most boring place in all the world!

Noah and Mrs Noah cross to URC

Noah (*rising*) Boys!
Mrs Noah (*clapping her hands*) Girls!

Reluctantly, the sons rise and cross to one window to listen to their father; their wives gather round the other window to listen to Mrs Noah. To make it clear that they are standing at windows, they open the shutters wide and the nearest person leans on the window-sill

Noah Shem! Ham! Japheth! Exciting news. The world ends in seven days! We must build an ark and escape across the seas! Quickly! Jump to it!

A pause. The sons think about this, then, as each one speaks, he moves away from the window

Shem I'm busy.
Ham So am I.
Japheth I'm so busy, busy, busy.
Shem (*sitting down inside the house*) Seed-time and harvest...
Ham (*sitting beside him*) Summer and winter...
Japheth (*lying down*) Day and night. So busy, busy, busy. (*He falls asleep*)
Noah (*pointing to each one in turn*) You chop. You saw. You hammer.
Sons Right, Father Noah!
Mrs Noah (*speaking to each of her daughters-in-law in turn*) You cut, you thread, you sew.
Wives Right, Mother Noah.

Noah's Ark

Quickly, everyone moves into position. The wives, with Mrs Noah, sit in a circle DS, creating the sail. Wife 1 cuts the cloth. Wife 2 threads the needle. Wife 3 and Mrs Noah sew the strips together

The sons work in a line US, with Noah. Shem chops down a tree; Ham saws another tree into planks and Japheth holds the planks in position while Noah nails them together to form the Ark around the platform

All this is done in mime, very precisely. While they work, the girls and boys in the chorus of Nasty Neighbours and Animals could sing a short song about Noah, or they could say:

Boys Chop, chop, chop.
Girls Snip, snip, snip…
All Working all day through.
Boys Saw, saw, saw.
Girls Sew, sew, sew.
All Still so much to do.
Boys Nail, nail, nail.
Girls Sail, sail, sail.
All Till our work is through.

Pause

Wife 1 Are you sure, Mrs Noah?
Mrs Noah Noah's sure. That's good enough for me.
Wife 2 I dread to think what the neighbours will say.
Wife 3 They'll say Noah's mad. And we're mad to obey him.
Mrs Noah Look, you're very young wives. You don't yet understand. Husbands dream. Wives … well, wives make those dreams come true.
Wives But if he's wrong?

The Nasty Neighbours come on stage. One group goes L of the women. They are curious, nosy. The wives and Mrs Noah try to ignore them. Another group goes R of the men. The sons and Noah ignore them. All this is mimed. Suddenly, the Nasty Neighbours realize what is happening

Group Two (*speaking to Noah and his sons*) You're building a ship!
Group One (*to the women*) You're making a sail!
Both Groups You must be mad!
Group Two Have you got planning permission for that?
Group One You want locking up!
Group Two You'll ruin our neighbourhood.
Group One What will people say?
Both Groups They'll think we're all mad!

During the following, in front of the platform, Ham and Japheth unfurl the strip of brown cloth—stored R *of the platform*

Group Two We don't want that great thing round here! Frightening our animals!
Group One We don't want people like you round here! Frightening our children!
Group Two Get out!
Group One Go on, clear off!

The Nasty Neighbours return very angrily to their places in the semi-circle. Ham and Japheth hold up the strip of brown cloth to represent the finished Ark. There is a long silence. Noah's sons and daughters-in-law are hurt and ashamed: it's horrible when people think your family are mad. Noah, standing URC, *tries to cheer them up*

Noah Cheer up, all of you. Look, it's finished.

Mrs Noah goes over to him and takes his arm, speaking very gently

Mrs Noah Noah, love.
Noah Time to move on.
Mrs Noah (*with a sigh*) Well, we can't stay here, that's for sure.

Noah's Ark

Noah Time to catch the animals, children!

The wives come forward, unhappily, and round up the Chorus of Animals. Each child represents a different wild animal—they can choose which one, but they must show us which animal they are by the way they stand and walk—not by any silly noises or painted masks! The animals are quickly rounded up and Shem shepherds them aboard the Ark, via the L end of the platform. For now, they remain out of sight, very quiet and very still, behind the brown cloth. Noah and Mrs Noah, standing together URC, arm in arm, watch the animals come aboard

Mrs Noah Our neighbours, Noah, they say you are mad. They call us fools for listening to you.
Noah (*stubbornly*) I don't care what they say. I care only what God says.
Mrs Noah And what *does* God say, Noah? What does God say we're to do *now*?
Noah (*suddenly sad*) I don't know.
Shem (*accusingly*) Build an ark, you said.
Ham That was easier said than done.
Japheth But we did it.
Wife 1 Catch the wild animals, you said.
Wife 2 Easier said than done, that was!
Wife 3 But we did it.
Sons What now?
Noah It's the end of the world!
Wives But when?
Noah Trust me!

They all freeze. Noah comes C, speaking to God

Speak to me, Lord. We're friends, you said. Friends talk to each other, don't they? Then why don't *you* talk to *me*? Our neighbours are talking. They call me mad, tell us we're all fools. They're laughing at us, Lord. Are you? (*He pauses*) All we need, Lord, is a sign, a signal. (*Shouting*) What are you waiting for? (*He suddenly realizes*) Are you, Lord, waiting too? Waiting for a signal from us? A sign that *we* trust *you*? (*He makes up his mind*) Right. (*He turns* us *to face his family*) All aboard!

They're not sure. They look at each other. Mrs Noah sighs deeply, then goes aboard. The wives and Shem follow. A silence. Everyone looks up. The Animals peep over the side of the Ark. Noah listens

Shem When's it going to start?

The Nasty Neighbours get up and come over to mock Noah and his family. Then they stop. They listen. They turn to face us. *They make the sounds of a strong wind. Then of rain*

Noah runs aboard

The Neighbours try to run away—running on the spot. The rain starts to pour down in big, heavy drops. The Neighbours soon get drenched. They can't run any more because the ground has turned to mud. They start to wade through the mud—still standing on one spot—at the same time using their hands to keep the rain off their heads

It rains even harder. They begin to be alarmed. The water reaches their knees. They can barely walk at all. They begin to be frightened

And still it rains. The water reaches their waists. In terror for their lives, now they have to launch out into the dark, swirling waters, and begin to swim—standing on one leg. Still it rains. They grow tired. Their arms ache. They're slowing down, starting to sink

At this point, the Ark begins to float. Shem and Ham are still holding the ends of the brown cloth and they move it gently up and down to suggest the Ark is moving over the waves

Everyone aboard sways very slightly, in time with the movement of the Ark

Noah's Ark 13

The Nasty Neighbours, drowning now, sink to the bottom of the sea and move, in slow motion, DC, where they sit, facing US, and watch the rest of the play, keeping up the sounds of the weather as necessary

(*Grumbling*) When's it going to stop?
Wife 1 Forty days and forty nights it's poured with rain!
Shem I'm soaked. We're all soaked—to the skin! The rain has washed away the land and every living thing. We're sick of this rain! When's it going to stop?

Suddenly, the sounds of the storm stop. A long silence

Noah Listen!
Mrs Noah It's stopped! The rain has stopped!
Ham We need fresh air to dry us. When's it going to start to blow?

The wind starts up gently—a wind created solely by the sounds made by the Nasty Neighbours—then builds until it howls

(*Grumbling*) When's it going to stop?
Wife 2 Forty days and forty nights the wind has howled.
Ham I'm dry as a bone. We're all dry as bones. The wind has blown away the sea!
Wife 2 And it's ruined my hair!
Ham We're sick of this wind! When's it going to stop?

Suddenly, the wind stops. A long silence

Mrs Noah It's stopped! The wind has stopped!

A terrible creak and then a splintering sound. The ship shudders. Everyone aboard shudders

Noah We've run aground! Dry ground!
Wife 3 *Wet* ground, you mean. Mud. Foul, stinking mud for miles and miles. We can't set foot on that!

Japheth We need bright sun to warm us. To dry up this stinking mud.
Noah Send out the dove. If there's any dry land out there, she'll find it!

One of the animals pulls out the dove, which was stored L of the platform, and flies off with it, swooping high and low, searching for dry land

Wife 3 Forty days. Forty days and forty nights we've waited.
Japheth In this boiling sun, this sweltering heat. Lord, I wish it would rain!
Mrs Noah Look! The dove! She's coming back!
Noah And in her beak—an olive branch!

The dove returns. The family cheers. The Ark cloth is lowered to the ground and left there

All ashore!

They disembark, gazing in wonder at the new world. The Animals move US, *gazing into the far distance, staying very still and facing* US. *Noah and his family come slightly* DS. *A bird sings*

Shem Listen!
Ham (*seeing a tree swaying in the breeze*) Look!
Japheth (*running a handful of soil through his fingers*) Feel!
Wife 1 It's all so beautiful!
Shem (*going over to her*) We can start again.
Wife 2 A Garden of Eden!
Ham (*going over to her*) From the very beginning.
Wife 3 A brave new world!
Japheth (*going over to her*) Just like it was before!

Suddenly, they remember. Suddenly, they are afraid

Wives Before…

Noah What is it?
Sons We're afraid!
Noah But why?
Wives What if it happens all over again?
Sons The Ark? The flood?

Noah comes DC

Noah Lord? They've kept their promise. They trusted me. I've kept my promise. I've trusted you. Please. Show us we have no more cause to fear.

God speaks, his voice this time provided by the Nasty Neighbours and the Animals to give it a really big, happy sound

God I promise. While the earth lasts, seed-time and harvest, cold and heat, summer and winter, day and night shall never cease.

The rainbow is revealed

This... I ... promise ... you!

If the play began with a song, it could end with the last verse sung again, while the actors come forward. Otherwise, the actors move quickly to the three sides of the audience, bow once, and then troop off UR and UL. As they do so, the Lights come up in the auditorium and go down on stage

THE END

FURNITURE AND PROPERTY LIST

On stage: Long boat-shaped brown cloth representing the Ark
Cut-out of dove mounted on short pole
Ladder with swathes of coloured cloth tied to it,
 representing a rainbow
Long strips of thin blue material representing rising water
Platform

GROUNDPLAN

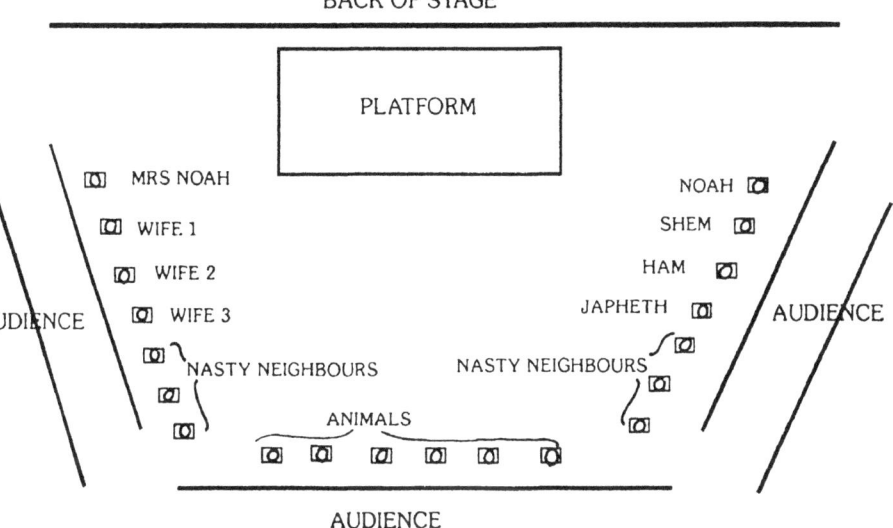

LIGHTING PLOT

Property fittings required: nil
Mixed mimed setting. The same throughout

Cue 1	**All** sit down	(Page 1)
	Fade down house lights, bring up stage lights	
Cue 2	**All** exit	(Page 15)
	Fade down stage lights, bring up house lights	

EFFECTS PLOT

No cues

www.ingramcontent.com/pod-product-compliance
Ingram Content Group UK Ltd.
Pitfield, Milton Keynes, MK11 3LW, UK
UKHW021849210426
5322IPUK00022B/550